TOOLS FOR CAREGIVERS

- **F&P LEVEL:** C
- **WORD COUNT:** 38
- **CURRICULUM CONNECTIONS:** animals, habitats, nature

Skills to Teach

- **HIGH-FREQUENCY WORDS:** a, for, has, in, it(s), this
- **CONTENT WORDS:** bat(s), big, bugs, cave, comes, ears, eats, eyes, flaps, fly, food, fruit, hang(s), looks, night, small, wings, yum
- **PUNCTUATION:** exclamation point, periods
- **WORD STUDY:** /k/, spelled c (*cave, comes*); long /e/, spelled ea (*ears, eats*); long /i/, spelled y (*fly*)
- **TEXT TYPE:** information report

Before Reading Activities

- Read the title and give a simple statement of the main idea.
- Have students "walk" through the book and talk about what they see in the pictures.
- Introduce new vocabulary by having students predict the first letter and locate the word in the text.
- Discuss any unfamiliar concepts that are in the text.

After Reading Activities

The letter "c" is used in two words in the book: "cave" and "come." It is a hard /c/, or /k/ sound in each word. What other words can readers think of that start with the letter c and have a /k/ sound? Write their answers on the board, such as "cat" or "car." Then ask readers to list words that have a soft /c/, or /s/ sound, such as "ice" or "pencil."

Tadpole Books are published by Jump!, 5357 Penn Avenue South, Minneapolis, MN 55419, www.jumplibrary.com

Copyright ©2024 Jump! International copyright reserved in all countries. No part of this book may be reproduced in any form without written permission from the publisher.

Editor: Jenna Gleisner **Designer:** Emma Almgren-Bersie

Photo Credits: CreativeNature_nl/iStock, cover; Nitin Chandra/Shutterstock, 1; All-stock-photos/Shutterstock, 2tl, 2bl, 3, 4–5; Gabriel Mendes/iStock, 2tr, 2ml, 10–11; Rudmer Zwerver/Shutterstock, 2mr, 2br, 8–9; Photoongraphy/Shutterstock, 6–7; Christian Ziegler/Minden Pictures/SuperStock, 12–13; ChameleonsEye/Shutterstock, 14–15; LedyX/Shutterstock, 16tl; Helga Madajova/Shutterstock, 16tr; Dennis Forster/Shutterstock, 16bl; Jukka Jantunen/Shutterstock, 16br.

Library of Congress Cataloging-in-Publication Data
Names: Deniston, Natalie, author.
Title: Bats / by Natalie Deniston.
Description: Minneapolis, MN: Jump!, Inc., [2024]
Series: My first animal books | Includes index.
Audience: Ages 3–6
Identifiers: LCCN 2023024565 (print)
LCCN 2023024566 (ebook)
ISBN 9798885246521 (hardcover)
ISBN 9798885246538 (paperback)
ISBN 9798885246545 (ebook)
Subjects: LCSH: Bats—Juvenile literature.
Classification: LCC QL737.C5 D46 2024 (print)
LCC QL737.C5 (ebook)
DDC 599.4—dc23/eng/20230530
LC record available at https://lccn.loc.gov/2023024565
LC ebook record available at https://lccn.loc.gov/2023024566

MY FIRST ANIMAL BOOKS

BATS

by Natalie Deniston

TABLE OF CONTENTS

Words to Know............................2

Bats......................................3

Let's Review!............................16

Index...................................16

WORDS TO KNOW

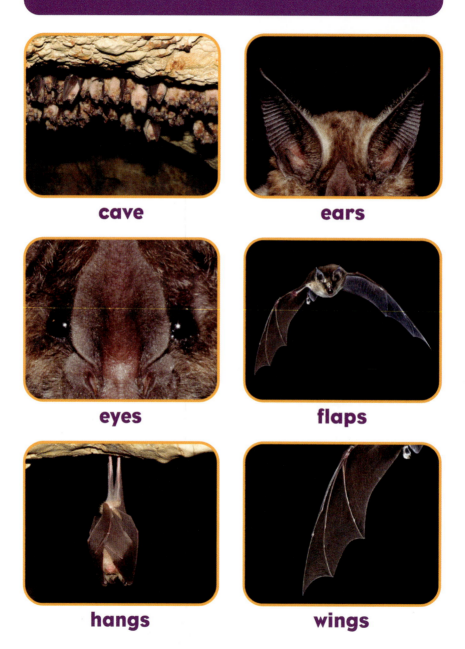

cave

ears

eyes

flaps

hangs

wings

BATS

A bat hangs.

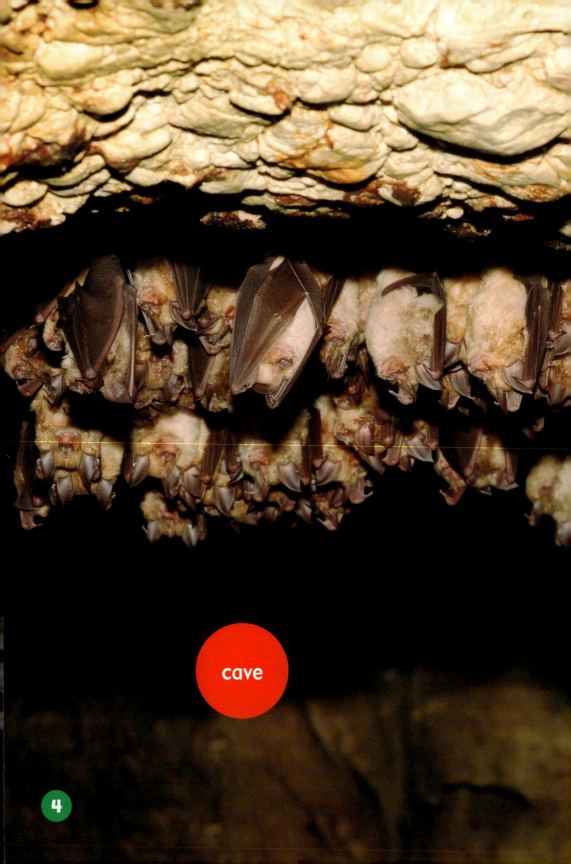

cave

Bats hang in a cave.

Night comes.

Bats fly.

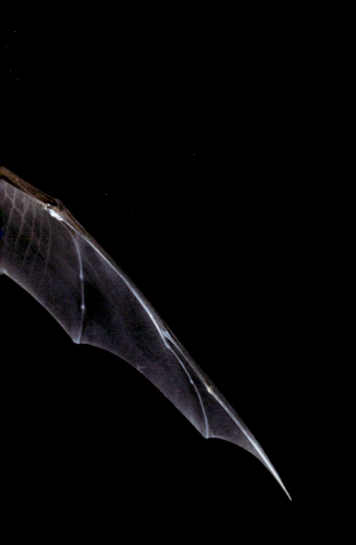

A bat flaps its wings.

It has big ears.

It has small eyes.

bug

It looks for food.

This bat eats fruit.

14

Yum!

LET'S REVIEW!

Bats have wings and can fly. Point to the other animals below that can fly.

INDEX

cave 5
ears 10
eats 13, 14
eyes 11

fly 7
hangs 3, 5
night 6
wings 9